Getting Started with Roo

Getting Started with Roo

Josh Long and Steve Mayzak

O'REILLY®

Beijing · Cambridge · Farnham · Köln · Sebastopol · Tokyo

Getting Started with Roo
by Josh Long and Steve Mayzak

Published by O'Reilly Media, Inc., 1005 Gravenstein Highway North, Sebastopol, CA 95472.

O'Reilly books may be purchased for educational, business, or sales promotional use. Online editions
are also available for most titles (*http://my.safaribooksonline.com*). For more information, contact our
corporate/institutional sales department: (800) 998-9938 or *corporate@oreilly.com*.

Editor:	Mike Loukides	**Cover Designer:**	Karen Montgomery
Production Editor:	Jasmine Perez	**Interior Designer:**	David Futato
Proofreader:	O'Reilly Production Services	**Illustrator:**	Robert Romano

ISBN: 978-1-449-30790-5

[LSI]

1312551249

Table of Contents

Preface

This is my first book with O'Reilly, and I'm very grateful for their help and encouragement. Their editorial team is first class, and efficient. It was great working with you.

I, like many of you, have been using Spring for a long, long time. I wasn't initially convinced I needed Spring Roo (to be honest). It wasn't until I sat with Ben Alex and Stefan Schmidt about a year ago and really started looking at it that I realized it was simply too valuable to ignore. There's a lot of power here and what really struck me was how that power didn't imply compromise: you can always go home again, and assert full control over your application. Eventually, you stop worrying about that at all, and just let Spring Roo do the work. One adage you hear a lot in the devops/build tool world is that, "your application is not a unique snowflake." That's true of infrastructure code, too. Spring Roo helps you bootstrap all that tedious infrastructure code, if you let it. It's like fast-forwarding a movie to the fun parts, quicker. It almost feels like cheating!

I want to thank my coauthor, Steve Mayzak, for all his help. We did this book and prepared a talk for OSCON, all in a very short space. It was a three-person job, but he took up the slack and got us to the finish line. Amazing work and I definitely owe you, kind sir.

I want to thank my wife, Richelle. She's learned, I think, that I am not a multitasking husband. Every now and then, I disappear into our home office and come back with a beard a week later (and, sometimes, some useful byproduct like a chapter or working code). It takes a patient, saintly woman to suffer that; she has, at every turn. Thanks, honey!

I want to thank Neo4J and Vaadin for their extra help on this book. Roo's powerful add-on architecture makes it very easy to look into new technologies because the cost to invest is so low, and iteration is very quick. Neo4j and Vaadin are two technologies that we cover in this book, but there are numerous other examples in the addon ecosystem, and I hope—if nothing else—that you'll explore.

Finally, thanks are owed to the Roo team, including Ben Alex, Stefan Schmidt, Alan Stewart, James Tyrrell, and Andrew Swan. The technology's wonderful, and it would not be but for their incredible dedication and hard work. Now, if you guys have any ideas about a Roo-Book-Preface-Writer add-on, I'd love to hear it...

—*Josh Long*

This being my first book, I looked to my fellow author, Josh, for help and guidance. Without him this book wouldn't be what it is so my heartfelt thanks goes out to him first and foremost.

My road to Spring Roo was not a direct one. Being a serious Grails fan, when I first heard about Spring Roo, I brushed it off as yet another RAD framework that couldn't possibly stand up to the mighty Grails! But, over time I was worn down by watching demo's, reading blogs about it and eventually trying it out myself. The first thing that impressed me was the Roo Shell, what a powerful tool. My first app with Roo was built with no manual, using only the hint feature in the shell to guide me. Before you knew it, I had a full blown Spring app up and running with UI, Validation and more. I was quickly becoming a fan. Long story short, I am now a huge Spring Roo fan and that is mostly what motivated me to write this book with Josh.

If you have followed a similar path to me, you will no doubt find a lot of power in with Spring Roo, just like I have. This short introduction to it will hopefully motivate you to dive deeper and possibly become an active contributor on the project. After all, a lot of the power in Spring Roo comes from addons and yours would be warmly welcomed. I happen to love the GWT and Vaadin addons but I'm more excited to see what comes next.

Before you move on, a little mush. I'd really like to thank my wife Jennifer and my daughter Makenzee for putting up with my hectic schedule lately. Coming up for air and spending time with them really makes it all worth it. "In the Face!!" girls! I know I said it before but seriously, Josh Long taught me a lot about writing, finding your voice and just getting it done so Josh, I owe ya and thanks.

—*Steve Mayzak*

Conventions Used in This Book

The following typographical conventions are used in this book:

Plain text
> Indicates menu titles, menu options, menu buttons, and keyboard accelerators (such as Alt and Ctrl).

Italic
> Indicates new terms, URLs, email addresses, filenames, file extensions, pathnames, directories, and Unix utilities.

`Constant width`
> Indicates commands, options, switches, variables, attributes, keys, functions, types, classes, namespaces, methods, modules, properties, parameters, values, ob-

jects, events, event handlers, XML tags, HTML tags, macros, the contents of files, or the output from commands.

`Constant width bold`

Shows commands or other text that should be typed literally by the user.

`Constant width italic`

Shows text that should be replaced with user-supplied values.

This icon signifies a tip, suggestion, or general note.

This icon indicates a warning or caution.

Using Code Examples

This book is here to help you get your job done. In general, you may use the code in this book in your programs and documentation. You do not need to contact us for permission unless you're reproducing a significant portion of the code. For example, writing a program that uses several chunks of code from this book does not require permission. Selling or distributing a CD-ROM of examples from O'Reilly books does require permission. Answering a question by citing this book and quoting example code does not require permission. Incorporating a significant amount of example code from this book into your product's documentation does require permission.

We appreciate, but do not require, attribution. An attribution usually includes the title, author, publisher, and ISBN. For example: "*Getting Started with Roo* by Josh Long and Steve Mayzak (O'Reilly). Copyright 2011 Josh Long and Steve Mayzak, 978-1-449-30790-5."

If you feel your use of code examples falls outside fair use or the permission given above, feel free to contact us at *permissions@oreilly.com*.

We'd Like to Hear from You

Please address comments and questions concerning this book to the publisher:

O'Reilly Media, Inc.
1005 Gravenstein Highway North
Sebastopol, CA 95472
(800) 998-9938 (in the United States or Canada)
(707) 829-0515 (international or local)

(707) 829-0104 (fax)

We have a web page for this book, where we list errata, examples, and any additional information. You can access this page at:

http://oreilly.com/catalog/9781449307905

To comment or ask technical questions about this book, send email to:

bookquestions@oreilly.com

For more information about our books, courses, conferences, and news, see our website at *http://www.oreilly.com*.

Find us on Facebook: *http://facebook.com/oreilly*

Follow us on Twitter: *http://twitter.com/oreillymedia*

Watch us on YouTube: *http://www.youtube.com/oreillymedia*

Safari® Books Online

Safari Books Online is an on-demand digital library that lets you easily search over 7,500 technology and creative reference books and videos to find the answers you need quickly.

With a subscription, you can read any page and watch any video from our library online. Read books on your cell phone and mobile devices. Access new titles before they are available for print, and get exclusive access to manuscripts in development and post feedback for the authors. Copy and paste code samples, organize your favorites, download chapters, bookmark key sections, create notes, print out pages, and benefit from tons of other time-saving features.

O'Reilly Media has uploaded this book to the Safari Books Online service. To have full digital access to this book and others on similar topics from O'Reilly and other publishers, sign up for free at *http://my.safaribooksonline.com*.

Acknowledgments

The authors would like to thank the Spring Roo team for such a wonderful project. We'd also like to thank Neo Technology and, in particular, Michael Hunger, whose contributions proved invaluable in the discussion of the Neo4j add-on.

CHAPTER 1

Your First Intrepid Hops ... err, Steps

Welcome! If you're reading this, then you've undoubtedly heard about Spring Roo from a friend or colleague, or perhaps you read about it online or saw a presentation about it. "Well, that's a presumptuous way to start a book!," I can imagine you thinking. I would, were I in your position.

But we've only just begun. In fact, I suspect that *most* people that read this book will come to it having been introduced to it from some other resource. Sure, most people aren't likely to just pick up a book *accidentally*, you might contend. But I'm willing to bet you picked this book up having heard quite a bit about Spring Roo a priori. This will be a common refrain: "My colleague was raving about Spring Roo and I just want to learn more ..."

This is natural. Most people—having heard claims of Roo's vaunted productivity and rapid turnaround times—will naturally assume they've not been told the whole story, that surely there must be a catch, even if what they heard was fantastic. It's only natural that one might attempt to investigate further, to clarify. One might seek trustworthy resources to light the way. You know O'Reilly—a good publisher, one that's never led you astray before.

And so, here we are.

You've got doubts. "If it sounds too good to be true..." But let me stop you right there! Spring Roo *does* sound too good to be true, but—as you'll see in short order—it's *not*.

The Pitch

Spring, the Most Productive Way to Build Java Applications

Spring Roo is a dynamic, domain-driven development framework from SpringSource, the makers of the insanely popular Spring framework, the de facto standard in enterprise Java. The Spring framework simplifies and expedites application development through a three-pronged approach: it enable services on plain-old-Java-objects (PO-

JOs) declaratively and transparently through dependency injection and aspect-oriented programming, and—where functionality can't be achieved effectively through those channels alone—it provides the simplest, cleanest abstractions and APIs under the sun to solve problems and to simplify existing, often verbose APIs.

If Spring's so popular, and so productive, then surely Roo is redundant? After all, what could it possibly hope to add? "Spring's the easiest way to work with Java today," you think, "you just said it yourself!"

Spring is no doubt the most proficient way to work with Java, but the current thinking strongly supports the conclusion that the next barrier to enhancing productivity on the JMV is the Java language itself.

This too is not news.

A Worthy Alternative

SpringSource is also the custodian of the open-source Grails project, which has similar goals as Spring Roo. Grails is a highly productive web development framework built on the Groovy language. The framework's built on top of Spring, but provides a work-flow that's far more like Ruby on Rails. Part of the productivity gains to be had in using this framework—part of its *power*—is that you can exploit the Groovy language's dynamism and conciseness. Groovy's a very dynamic language. It supports meta programming and the creation of exotic domain-specific languages. These features alone can pack quite a punch! They let the Grails developer specify more in far fewer lines of code than a Java developer could hope to achieve.

For some people, Grails is a compelling option, and the goal of Roo isn't to take away from that. For some, however, Grails simply isn't an option. Perhaps they can't use Groovy in their environment, or they don't want to make the large jump to Grails, feeling perfectly comfortable with their existing Spring and Java skills.

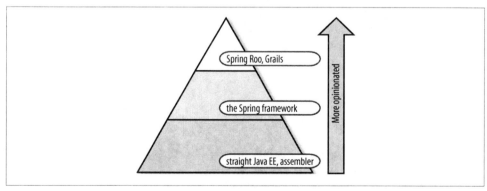

Figure 1-1. Pyramid of opinionation

Spring Roo Means No Compromises

Spring Roo is built using standard Java. You object, "But you just said … !" (I'm getting to that, hold on!) Spring Roo uses standard Java and Spring, but during development time, the Spring Roo shell watches you work, helping out as possible and required. Think of Spring Roo as being the ultimate pair-programming buddy, or the most advanced code completion you've ever seen.

As an example of this power, suppose you're in the middle of editing a JPA entity in a Spring Roo project, and adding a field of interest—perhaps a `dateOfBirth` field to a `Customer` entity. As soon as you've finished typing out the field definition, Spring Roo automatically jumps in and adds a corresponding accessor and mutator pair for that field to a shadow class definition in the background. Similarly, it will implement a `toString()` definition (reflecting the fields added) if one does not already exist, and it will implement an `equals()` method following the same criteria. This assistance isn't a one shot, either; it's intelligent. If you update the field, the accessor and mutator are updated as well as the `equals` and `toString` methods. If you add an equals method to the JPA entity, the shadow definition is removed, delegating to your implementation instead. So, this shadow class definition is kept in sync, responding to your changes, but it does not get in your way. It defers to your will in all cases.

What is this shadow definition you ask? Well, it's an AspectJ Inter Type Declaration (ITD) that Spring Roo maintains in the background. When your application compiles, the ITD is merged with the Java code, creating one class that has both the field you typed in, as well as the automatically generated accessor and mutator pair, a correct `equals()` implementation, and a correct `toString()` implementation. So, you write Java code, and Spring Roo augments the Java code with AspectJ Inter-Type Declarations (ITDs). You should never need to modify these ITD definitions. However, if you do decide to make modifications, do so at your own peril, as Spring Roo reserves the right to remove or modify them at will.

So, you get Java, but you don't have to pay the cost of writing all that Java. For every line you write, Spring Roo will happily write any number of other boilerplate lines to relieve you of the burden. Because it is just code-generated Java and Spring, and nothing else, it's as performant, well-written, and nicely architected as possible. Spring Roo is opinionated, but it always defers to you first.

Indeed, Spring Roo will never do anything unless you explicitly ask for it. It's entirely *opt-in*—there's no need to spend time undoing Spring Roo's decisions. In the above example, we could bring Spring Roo into the project by explicitly directing it to do something for us from the shell, or by using compile-time retention-only annotations on our classes. If we did that, Spring Roo will monitor our workspace, using the annotations as a cue to intercede on our behalf, working in tandem with you in a background shadow definition.

Spring Roo's very conducive to round tripping because of the aforementioned intelligence in the code generation. It's possible to build your application entirely using Spring

Roo. However, it may be that you eventually need to take your application out of Spring Roo's sweet spot. Perhaps you've simply gotten 90% of your Spring application done, and want to take it the last 10% yourself. Here, too, Roo is different. You can completely remove Spring Roo from your application using push-in refactoring, yielding a generic Spring and Java-only web application that looks exactly as if you'd written it yourself and behaves exactly as it did when Spring Roo was managing its development.

This brings us around to the final piece of the puzzle: the development environment. After all, "refactoring" connotes IDEs, tooling, and Java development. And well it should! You already know that Spring Roo's a shell that sits and monitors your code as you work, helping out wherever it can, passively, but what about these ITDs? The ITDs that it creates are not valid Java—they comply with the AspectJ language and can't be compiled directly using `javac`. This is an easier problem to overcome than you might imagine. First, both Eclipse (in conjunction with the AspectJ Development Toolkit (ADJT) which is bundled with Eclipse and with SpringSource Tool Suite) as well as IntelliJ IDEA support the ITD format. As a result, when you work with Spring Roo projects, you still have access to code completion and to the refactoring support you'd expect. Those shadow definition accessors and mutators we created earlier will still show up in the code completion prompt in your favorite IDE. Additionally, every Spring Roo project ships with a correctly configured Maven build that automatically processes the code at compile time, so everything builds correctly.

Getting Started

The Tooling

Spring Roo is based on the sophisticated interplay between several moving parts. To do its work, Spring Roo needs to play a role during your development, and it must be there to help during compilation. This means you need a correctly configured development tool, and a correctly configured build process and test environment, beyond Spring Roo itself. This, as it turns out, is pretty easy to fix. In this section, we'll set up the SpringSource Tool Suite (STS), a free development environment from SpringSource, based on Eclipse. The SpringSource Tool Suite's got lots of extra features that makes working with Spring and the sister projects dead simple. Beyond being a particularly nice environment for Spring development, it's also loaded to the gills with conveniences and useful-to-have packages. SpringSource Tool Suite always follows the main releases of Eclipse pretty closely, but integrates numerous plugins that can be a pain to set up independently, but that most people have to set up, anyway, like the Maven M2Eclipse plugin, or plugins for various source-code management options that aren't included by default. It is effectively a subset of the Eclipse IDE for Java EE Developers, with a large superset of functionality integrated to reflect the realities of modern day enterprise Java development. We'll use it throughout the book because it represents the path of least resistance and it's a very capable choice, as well!

Because Spring Roo takes away so much of the boilerplate code, it is possible to develop Spring Roo applications using only a text editor and the Roo shell running in the background. Of course, we wouldn't recommend it, but you *could*! Users of IntelliJ will be happy to know that the latest version of IntelliJ IDEA (the premium version) also supports Spring Roo development.

Let's first obtain the SpringSource Tool Suite:

1. Go to *http://www.springsource.com/developer/sts*, and then click on "Download STS," on the bottom right (Figure 1-2).

2. Install the distribution appropriate to your environment: there are builds for OSX (both Carbon and Cocoa, 32 and 64 bit), Linux, and Windows (Figure 1-3).

3. Once installed, you'll have everything you need to be productive, quickly!

Figure 1-2. STS download page

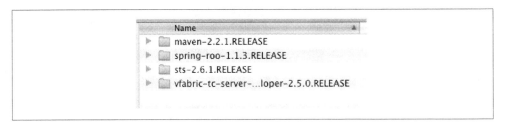

Figure 1-3. Layout of STS folder

By default, the SpringSource Tool Suite comes integrated with Maven, Spring Roo, and the Developer Edition of SpringSource's tcServer. SpringSource's tcServer is a hardened, more robust distribution of the leading Apache Tomcat web server. The Developer Edition also includes integrated monitoring and analysis of your application in a package called Spring Insight, which lets you dissect the performance of your running Spring applications at fine granularity.

Our first Spring Roo application

Let's dig in by building something simple—you know, to kick the tires a bit.

Building a CRM is a rite of passage for every application developer today. We've all written one at some point or another. If pressed, we suspect most developers would admit to having done it—at least once (in college, perhaps? You don't have to admit it aloud. You were young. It was a warm summer evening ... the moon was full ... and your awesome new startup (TM) needed a way to manage customer data. Totally cool. No worries. We won't judge.)

Now that you've got SpringSource Tool Suite installed, fire it up, select a workspace, and then go to File > New > Spring Roo Project (Figure 1-4).

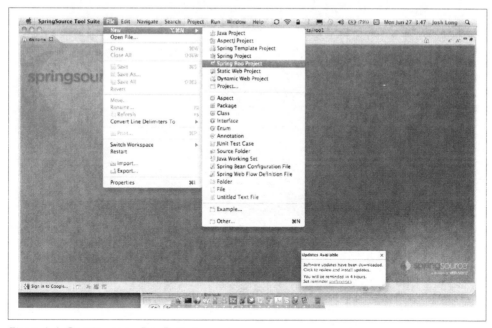

Figure 1-4. Opening a new Roo Project

The dialog's a bit "busy," but you don't need to worry about most of it. This wizard simply dumps its inputs into a command line invocation, which you could do directly

---

as well. Only fill out the first two fields—the rest you can leave as the defaults for the large majority of the time.

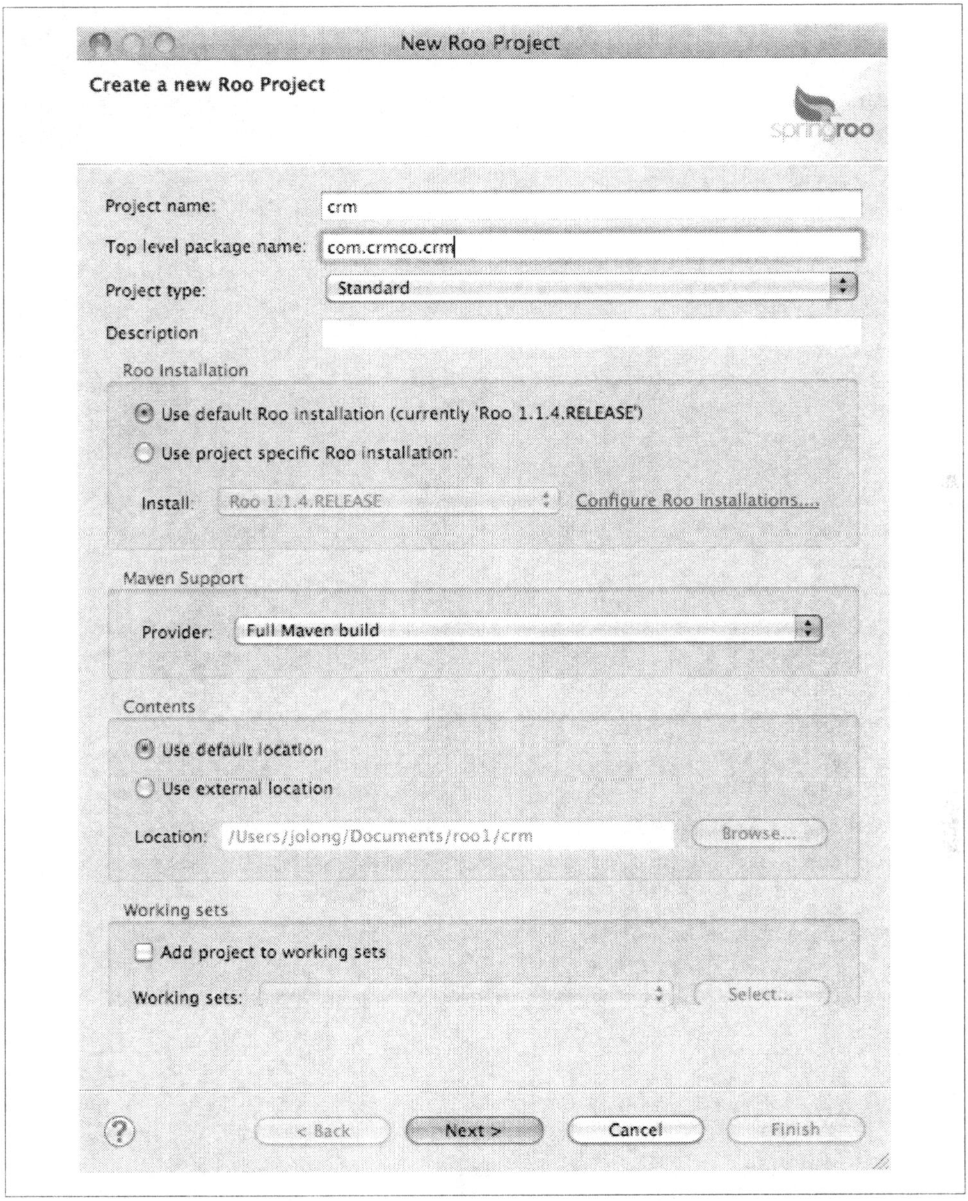

Figure 1-5. Creating a new Roo Project

Click "Next," and then click "Finish." After a flash of activity, this will dump you into the Spring Source Tool Suite with a fresh Spring project, based on Maven.

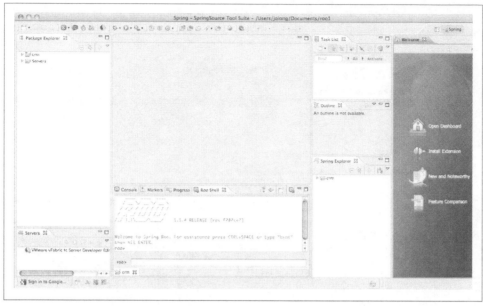

Figure 1-6. Spring Source Tool Suite with a fresh Roo Project

As you examine the workspace, you can see there's a Roo Shell at the bottom of the screen. On the left is your freshly created project. First thing that you'll notice is that it's got a simple directory structure that confirms with the directory structure used in Maven builds. This project *is* a Maven project.

Directory	Description
src/main/java	Where your Java code is to be stored. The code in this directory are to be included in your final build artifact.
src/main/resources	Where things that should be reference-able from the root of the classpath should be stored. This includes META-INF folders and other non-.class files that you intend to be bundled with the final archive artifact.
src/test/java	Where your Java-based test code lives. This code will not be in the final build archive, but it will be evaluated before your code's built.
src/test/resources	This serves the same role as the src/main/resources folder, except it exists only while the unit test code in src/test/java is being evaluated.

Maven projects defined their dependencies in a file called pom.xml that lives at the root of the project. Dependencies defined in pom.xml are automatically synchronized with the Eclipse project as classpath dependencies (you can inspect them in the project properties dialog or simply click on the "Maven Dependencies" Eclipse Classpath Container) thanks to the M2Eclipse plugin which comes bundled with SpringSource Tool Suite out of the box. As you enable features with Spring Roo, it will modify your pom.xml file and add dependencies as required. This is all automatic, and behind the scenes. The Maven file already represents a sophisticated build. A fresh Roo project already has JUnit, the correct and latest versions of Spring, AspectJ, logging, and the latest servlet APIs. Not bad! We'll revisit this pom.xml as we build our application, so let's get back to building our CRM.

Spring Roo applications are *domain driven*, everything you do stems from your domain objects, your entity objects. You describe your domain objects to Spring Roo and it will handle building persistence code (using JPA 2.0), web application code to manipulate those entities, and much more.

Don't take my word for it, though. If you ever have a question, simply ask Spring Roo! Sometimes knowing that there is an answer is as good as knowing the answer. If you're ever in doubt as to what Spring Roo can help you achieve, type "help," and then hit Enter. Spring Roo will show all the commands that it can respond to. Similarly, if you ever have a doubt as to how to proceed, ask Roo by typing "hint" on the shell. Let's do so:

```
Welcome to Spring Roo. For assistance press CTRL+SPACE or type "hint" then hit ENTER.

roo> hint
Roo requires the installation of a JPA provider and associated database.
Type 'persistence setup' and then hit CTRL+SPACE three times.
We suggest you type 'H' then CTRL+SPACE to complete "HIBERNATE".
After the --provider, press CTRL+SPACE twice for database choices.
For testing purposes, type (or CTRL+SPACE) HYPERSONIC_IN_MEMORY.
If you press CTRL+SPACE again, you'll see there are no more options.
As such, you're ready to press ENTER to execute the command.
Once JPA is installed, type 'hint' and ENTER for the next suggestion.
roo>
```

See? Everything's about the domain objects—it wants you to set up the persistence infrastructure. So, oblige the shell—type in "persistence setup," and then type CTRL + SPACE. If you're using Roo from the shell inside of SpringSource Tool Suite, then the shell can offer you autocompletion using the same key commands as you'd use in the Java code editor. On a standard operating system shell, you'd use TAB, instead, just as you would to autocomplete commands in Bash, for example.

The code completion for the persistence setup command offers two options, both of which are required—one for --database, and one for --provider. Any code completion options that you get when you type CTRL + SPACE are required. Once you've selected a required code completion (like "persistence setup --database"), type CTRL + SPACE again to see if Roo has suggested values for that option. In this case, there are several different suggested values for --database. For expedience, I recommend you choose "H2_IN_MEMORY." Hit CTRL + SPACE again, and the only remaining, required option ("--provider"), will be added to the command line. Type CTRL + SPACE again to get suggested values for the "--provider" option. Again, there are several options here, as well. One well-known option is "HIBERNATE" and unless you have a preference, go ahead and select it.

Often, commands may have optional arguments that you can use to fine tune the results. To see the optional arguments for any command, type "--," and then type CTRL + TAB to see a full list of possibilities. Hit Enter.

The shell will flash and you'll see telltale signs that Roo has added several new dependencies to your `pom.xml` in service of your request, including Hibernate, the Hibernate JPA 2.0 implementation, Commons Pool, Commons DBCP, the Hibernate JSR 303 (Java Bean Validation) implementation, and several Spring dependencies, including the Spring JDBC and transaction support. It's also added a JPA persistence entity information file (`src/main/resources/META-INF/persistence.xml`), as well as Spring application context (in `src/main/resources/META-INF/spring/applicationContext.xml`). Finally, the Roo command has added a repository to the Maven `pom.xml` where new dependencies can be found.

Sure, the narrative of these last few paragraphs has taken more than a few minutes of your life, but the code—from nothing, to this point, has taken an almost trivial amount of effort. Let's keep rolling and build our model.

The model is simple enough to be approachable, but complex enough that we can see how Spring Roo handles common scenarios. We won't reprint all the Roo commands here, just enough so that you can see how to begin—the rest are easy to piece together.

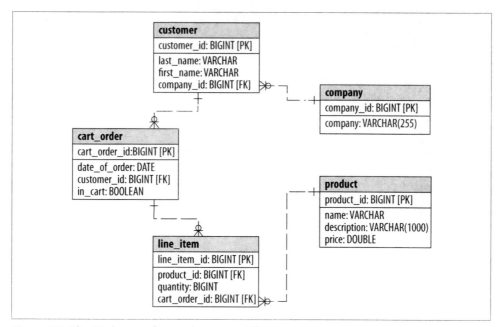

Figure 1-7. The ER diagram for our domain model

Roo supports a few different workflows when building your domain objects using JPA. For greenfield domains, you can declaratively build your entities using the Spring Roo command line. We'll build the model above using this approach. You should know that Spring Roo also supports reverse engineering existing domain models from a database (a feature called "database reverse engineering," commonly abbreviated as "DBRE") and generating the appropriate JPA entities. We'll look at this approach shortly. Finally, there's no reason you can't mix 'n match these workflows: perhaps you will bootstrap your Spring Roo application using DBRE, but then use Spring Roo to maintain and evolve those entities.

As we are working, Roo is keeping track of our commands and writing them to a log at the root of the project in a file called log.roo which you can refer to anytime you want. Naturally, you can also save off the commands into a file and run them on the shell, effectively replaying your commands. This is, among other things, a very convenient way to bootstrap new projects.

We're going to tell you how to do this, *this time*, but remember, long after you've finished reading this tidy, tiny tome on Spring Roo, you may occasionally find that you're confused on the precise syntax or command options. Again, "hint" is your best friend here. It'll guide the way.

To create an entity in Spring Roo, simply type "ent," and then hit CTRL + TAB. It'll auto-complete the command for you, filling in "entity" as well as the first and only required option, "--class." Here you need to specify a class to use.

Recall that the first step of the process was to fill out the Spring Roo dialog, specifying a Project Name and a Top Level Package Name. The Top Level Package Name is the root package of your application. For instance, you might have a package, com.crmco.crm, that prefixes all parts of your application; the domain model lives in com.crmco.crm.model, the web-tier specific code lives in com.crmco.crm.web, etc. Roo seizes upon this convention and enshrines it in the idea of the Top Level Package Name. You can use the tilde character ("~") as shorthand for the Top Level Package Name. It'll be automatically replaced with the appropriate value whenever it's referenced, in very much the same way as the tilde character is commonly substituted for the $HOME environment variable on Unixes.

So, for our Customer entity, simply specify "~.model.Customer" as the value for the --class option, and Roo will create a new JPA entity class com.crmco.crm.model.Customer.

Hit Enter and Roo will list the files that it has changed or created in response to your command:

```
roo> entity --class ~.model.Customer
Created SRC_MAIN_JAVA/com/crmco/crm/model
Created SRC_MAIN_JAVA/com/crmco/crm/model/Customer.java
Created SRC_MAIN_JAVA/com/crmco/crm/model/Customer_Roo_Configurable.aj
Created SRC_MAIN_JAVA/com/crmco/crm/model/Customer_Roo_Entity.aj
```

```
Created SRC_MAIN_JAVA/com/crmco/crm/model/Customer_Roo_ToString.aj
~.model.Customer roo>
```

A couple of things are striking about this output.

First, the prompt has changed. It was "roo>," and now it's "~.model.Customer roo>." The prompt indicates the *focus*. The focus describes the subject of actions on the shell. In this case, Roo has given the entity you've just created focus. It knows that, more than likely, subsequent commands will attempt to modify this entity, and that it would be inconvenient if you had to specify the entity each time.

Second, Roo gave you four files, not just a single one! The first file (SRC_MAIN_JAVA/com/crmco/crm/model/Customer.java) you might correctly recognize as the Java class for your Customer JPA entity. It looks like this:

```
package com.crmco.crm.model;
import org.springframework.roo.addon.entity.RooEntity;
import org.springframework.roo.addon.javabean.RooJavaBean;
import org.springframework.roo.addon.tostring.RooToString;

@RooJavaBean
@RooToString
@RooEntity
public class Customer {
}
```

Kind of underwhelming, huh? Not a lot here. The only thing of interest here are the annotations at the top. These annotations are compile-time retention only—they disappear once the code's compiled. They are used to signal to Roo that you want Roo to manage boilerplate code for you while you are developing. This boilerplate code exists in the other .aj files that were created.

You can click on the shell to open the other files, those ending in .aj. These files are the AspectJ ITDs we mentioned earlier. You won't be able to see them in the Eclipse Package Explorer unless you disable a filter. To do so, click on the little down-arrow on the Package Explorer, choose Filters, and then find the checkbox for "Hide gener ated Spring Roo ITDs" (Figure 1-8). Uncheck it if it's selected.

You are not supposed to modify these other files, they are there for Roo but lets see whats in them. Open the SRC_MAIN_JAVA/com/crmco/crm/model/Cus tomer_Roo_Entity.aj file. This file exists because Spring Roo placed a @RooEntity annotation on your class. If you examine the code, you'll see that Spring Roo's already generated an ID for your Customer entity, it's already generated a version column, *and* it's already generated simple, ActiveRecord-style CRUD methods to create, remove, update, and delete a Customer object using a JPA EntityManager. If you examine the other file (Customer_Roo_ToSring.aj), you'll see that Spring Roo knows about the instance variables in the class—including the ID and the version column—and already incorporates them into a useful toString() definition. The last file (Customer_Roo_Con figurable.aj) simply adds the AspectJ @Configurable annotation to the entity so that Spring can transparently inject the JPA EntityManager into the entity class. Spring has

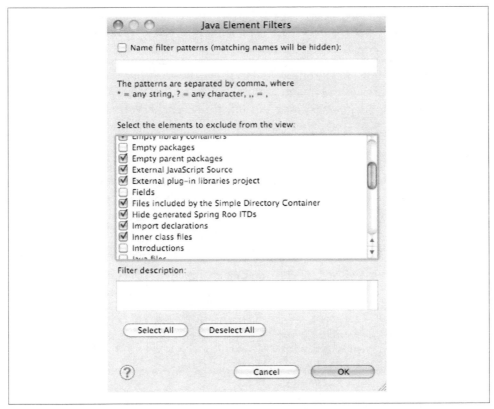

Figure 1-8. Disabling a filter

no problems injecting collaborating beans into other Spring beans that it instantiates in the application context. Because Spring doesn't control the construction and lifecycle of the JPA `Customer` entity—it needs to use AspectJ, which `@Configurable` specifically supports.

A quick word about Roo's (neighborly, but sometimes unsolicited) help: it's entirely optional. For example, if you feel like you have a lot to offer in `toString` method implementations, and want to provide your own, then you can do so. Add a `toString` method implementation in your Customer.java class and the corresponding `Customer_Roo_ToString.aj` file will disappear! Spring Roo will *never* presume to know more than you. At the first sign that you want to drive, to exert control over the code, Roo will get out of the way. If you simply don't want Roo to even bother, simply remove the annotation from the `Customer.java` file and watch as Spring Roo removes the corresponding `.aj` file. If, later, you decide you that you were a bit hasty in dismissing its help, simply replace the annotation and Roo will obediently hop back into action again.

Let's get back to it. We'll define the column for the first name and the last name. To create the attribute, use the Roo `field` command, like this:

```
field string --fieldName lastName --notNull
```

Spring Roo will automatically add a field to the `Customer.java` class and it'll generate corresponding accessors and mutators in the `Customer_Roo_Entity.aj` file. It also updates the `Customer_Roo_ToString.aj` to include the new field. Very smooth! You type a field, and Roo contorts to welcome that new field into the code base, updating everything as appropriate.

You could simply add the field to the entity class, if you'd like. In this case, it turns out to be roughly the same amount of typing so it really is a matter of choice. The Roo shell command has other options that you may not remember how to set up manually, which makes the Spring Roo command more convenient. For the lastName field, simply add it, manually:

```
@NotNull private String lastName;
```

Just as last time, Spring Roo hops into action, changing the other code as required to welcome the new field. See? Roo's flexible. It gets out of your way and helps whenever it can.

So far, so good! Admittedly, this is a very simple entity so far. Let's set up the `CartOrder` entity, which has a one-to-many relationship with the `Customer` entity. First, create the `CartOrder` entity, just as you did the `Customer` entity:

```
entity --class ~.model.CartOrder
field boolean --fieldName inCart
field date --fieldName dateOfOrder
```

To link the two, we need to use a special variant of the field command to establish the one-to-many relationship from the `Customer`, to the `CartOrders`. Let's go back to our Customer entity and manipulate it.

Type:

```
focus --class ~.model.Customer
```

to change back to the `Customer` entity. Then, define the collection:

```
field set --fieldName orders --type ~.model.CartOrder --cardinality ONE_TO_MANY --
mappedBy customer
```

This is half of our relationship, but we have to define the reverse side of the relationship, too. The "mappedBy" attribute tells Spring Roo that the field to use on the `CartOrder` entity is the customer attribute, presumably of type `Customer`. This is how you map a foreign key—the inverse side of this relationship—in JPA. Focus on the `CartOrder`, again, and then add the reference to the owning side—a `Customer` entity:

```
focus --class ~.model.CartOrder
field reference --fieldName customer --type ~.model.Customer --cardinality MANY_TO_ONE
```

Database Reverse Engineering

It would be easy to continue in this way, fleshing out the balance of the model. Instead, however, let's look at Spring Roo's database reverse engineering feature (DBRE) to simply generate the model for us from an existing schema.

```
database reverse engineer --package ~.domain --schema PUBLIC
```

The command will fail because it can't figure out which driver to use to connect to the database from which the domain model should be generated, but Spring Roo knew this might arise and has provided guidance. When you issue the command, it'll respond that you need to install a driver for the database, and then show results:

```
database reverse engineer --package ~.domain --schema PUBLIC

Located add-on that may offer this JDBC driver
1 found, sorted by rank; T = trusted developer; R = Roo 1.1 compatible
ID T R DESCRIPTION
-------------------------------------------------------------------------
01 Y Y 1.3.155.0020 H2 #jdbcdriver driverclass:org.h2.Driver. This bundle...
-------------------------------------------------------------------------
[HINT] use 'addon info id --searchResultId ..' to see details about a search result
[HINT] use 'addon install id --searchResultId ..' to install a specific search result,
or
[HINT] use 'addon install bundle --bundleSymbolicName TAB' to install a specific add-
on version
JDBC driver not available for 'org.h2.Driver'
```

You heard the man ... err ... shell! Get hopping! It's practically rolled the red carpet:

```
addon install id --searchResultId 01
```

Spring Roo will try to connect to the H2 database instance and look for tables to generate the entities from. It won't find any, of course. You need to install the tables, which are available as part of this book's source code download, as roo_crm.sql. In our local installation, we're running the H2 database as a server, not in-memory. You can see what database properties Roo's already using by using the database properties list command (which simply dumps the values in src/main/resources/META-INF/spring/database.properties).

Our local configuration looks like this:

```
database.password=
database.url=jdbc:h2:tcp://localhost/~/roo_crm
database.username=sa
database.driverClassName=org.h2.Driver
```

In this configuration, the H2 client will try to connect to an H2 database instance running as a server, locally. You can download the H2 database from www.h2database.com (*http://www.h2database.com*). Unzip it where you'd like and the run the h2.bat or h2.sh script inside the bin folder.

Change the H2 database connection URL like this:

```
database properties set --key database.url --value jdbc:h2:tcp://localhost/~/roo_crm
```

It'll churn for a second, and then return you to the shell, at which point you can simply re-issue the database reverse engineering command. Note that we've specified ~.domain, not ~.model, to avoid having the DBRE command overwrite, and conflict with, the existing Customer class definition. You may simply delete the existing ~.model package.

 "I Need To See Your ID" Be sure that your tables have a primary key. Roo requires a primary key (and also really, really likes a version column —some addons don't work without it) to do its work, so make sure that you've got one on all tables you import. Some recommended guidelines: use a long or equivalent type for the ID, and at least an integer for the version column. This will please Roo (and make your queries faster).

The entities that are brought in from the DBRE process are empty—all the fields that were generated are in an ITD—of the form $ENTITY_Roo_DbManaged.aj.

If you're confident in the reverse engineering, then open up the $ENTITY_Roo_DbManaged.aj file and move all the fields into the entity directly. This will cause the $ENTITY_Roo_DbManaged.aj file to be deleted, and works more naturally when adding finder methods, as we describe in the next section.

Riddle Me This

Thus far, we've simply built our entities and relied on the generated query methods that are added to them by default. We can, for example, interact with our database using the methods added to each of our entities by default:

```
// create a new Customer entity
Customer customer = new Customer() ;
customer.setFirstName("steve");
customer.setLastName("mayzak");
customer.persist();

// presumably we've gotten ahold of the ID
Customer steve = Customer.findCustomer( 1L ) ;
steve.setFirstName( "Steve" );
steve.setLastName( "Mayzak" );
steve.merge() ;

// count the records in the database
long customers = Customer.countCustomers();
```

This is a start, but often we need to retrieve data using more sophisticated queries. To do this in Spring Roo, we need to create "finder" methods. This, as it turns out, is very easy. Spring Roo has a whole arsenal of finders that it knows how to generate without your help at all. First consult this list to see if any of the ones it can add are what you're looking for:

```
~.domain.Customer roo> focus --class ~.domain.Customer
~.domain.Customer roo> finder list
findCustomersByCartOrders(Set cartOrders)
findCustomersByCompanyId(Company companyId)
findCustomersByFirstNameEquals(String firstName)findCustomersByFirstNameIsNotNull()
findCustomersByFirstNameIsNull()
findCustomersByFirstNameLike(String firstName)
findCustomersByFirstNameNotEquals(String firstName)
findCustomersByLastNameEquals(String lastName)
findCustomersByLastNameIsNotNull()
findCustomersByLastNameIsNull()
findCustomersByLastNameLike(String lastName)
findCustomersByLastNameNotEquals(String lastName)
~.domain.Customer roo>
```

Use the `finder add` command, specifying the finder name as specified in the `finder list` output:

```
~.domain.Customer roo> finder add --finderName findCustomersByFirstNameLike
```

Open up the newly created Customer_Roo_Finder.aj file to inspect the finder method that was created for you.

If you don't see a finder that you want already, you can of course simply add a finder as you'd like in the entity's Java class, in the same style as the finders generated by Spring Roo.

On The (Active) Record

Spring Roo builds *active record* style entity objects. Active record objects—from Martin Fowler's active record pattern—are essentially entity objects whose interface includes methods to store, retreive (through queries, or by ID), update, and delete the entity. While the active record pattern is famously used quite succesfully in Ruby on Rails and Grails, it's little known in typical enterprise Java shops where the preferred approach is to use services, or, as often, services *and* repositories. It is still easy to build a service tier facade with Spring Roo, delegating to the active record-style entities to perform basic repository object duties.

Persistence with Spring Data Graph

Has always featured great support for JPA, and—with a newly revised, more generic meta-model available to addon developers, you can expect Spring Roo to support alternative persistence models.

This is becoming valuable as companies are increasingly faced with more complex or higher volume data challenges. There is a new breed of database—iconified by the name "NOSQL" (Not-Only-SQL). NOSQL is all about pragmatism—use the best tool for the job, and—to use a cliche—understanding that one size does *not* fit all. When we talk about persistence challenges that use a hybrid architecture consisting of both the new generation of databases, and more traditional RDBMSes, we call it "polyglot persistence."

The Spring Data project embraces and simplifies NOSQL technologies and provides idiomatic Spring support for the various technologies, including template implementations, exception translation, mapping and conversion support, and much more.

Spring Data is an umbrella project. There is distinct support for all manner of technologies, including key-value stores (e.g., Redis), document stores (e.g., MongoDB), and graph stores (e.g., Neo4j), among others.

In this section, we'll look at a Roo addon for Spring Data Graph—which brings the power of Neo4j to your Spring applications. Neo4j is an open-source, Java graph database that has been available since 2003, and is in use in production in companies worldwide. The Spring Roo addon was developed by Neo4j, in cooperation with the Spring Data and Spring Roo teams.

Graph Databases are the most flexible of the available NOSQL solutions. They store your data as a graph of nodes and relationships both having properties. This maps naturallly to what most people imagine when they build their entity domain models. You can see that object networks map directly to a graph without having to deal with object-relational management pains like impedance mismatch. Most graph databases are schema free and embrace your data as it is, without bending it to fit their constraints.

In the end, everything is connected and the relationships between things are often more important than the things themselves. It's not hard to think of examples that are better served by these kinds of topologies: social networks, computer networks, inventory management or e-commerce solutions all spring to mind. Graph databases excel at heavily interconnected data. They invite you to add more relationships and properties to enrich your data model with all information available. This very rich data model invites you to explore and traverse the graph to find answers to your questions. Perhaps even to questions you didn't know you had.

Graph traversals are local operations which are independent of data set size and extremely fast. Even on commodity hardware, Neo4j can traverse millions of nodes in mere milliseconds regardless of dataset size.

Spring Data Graph comes with an object graph mapping technology that uses conventions and some annotations (much like JPA) and leverages AspectJ under the hood to provide a transparent mapping between your POJOs and the graph database. Entities are mapped to nodes in the graph, references to other entities are mapped to relationships. You even have the ability to map relationships to real entities (Relationship Entity) that provides a much richer way of working with them. All fields of an entity or relationship are mapped to properties of the graph elements. Spring Data Graph also stores type information inside the graph which allows you to retrieve any node and automatically get it back as instance of the correct type. But as the graph is schema-less you can also project nodes to other, unrelated types that share properties with the initial one. AspectJ is also used to add some Active Record like operations to each entity—just as we saw earlier, in the JPA examples.

Spring Data Graph is also able to integrate with a JPA application—this is called cross-store persistence or polyglot persistence. This support lets you have the best of both worlds: store your line of business data in a traditional RDBMS, but store the data about the relationships in Neo4j.

Let's dive directly into action and see how the plugin is installed and used. Spring Roo addons make it even easier to set up your NOSQL project. To install the Neo4j addon, you need to use the Roo Bot the plugin management solution for Spring Roo. Let's go to the Roo shell and search for the add-on and install it. You probably have to trust my pgp key first, like this:

```
roo> pgp trust --keyId 0x29C2D8FD
```

Added trust for key:

```
>>>> KEY ID: 0x29C2D8FD <<<<
    More Info: http://keyserver.ubuntu.com/pks/lookup?
fingerprint=on&op=index&search=0x29C2D8FD
        Created: 2011-Jan-06 10:48:11 +0000
        Fingerprint: 558eb0489fe5500c68fa8a306107f33d29c2d8fd
        Algorithm: RSA_GENERAL
        User ID: Michael Hunger <Michael.Hunger@jexp.de>
            Signed By: Key 0x29C2D8FD (Michael Hunger <Michael.Hunger@jexp.de>)
        Subkey ID: 0xDEFB5FB1 [RSA_GENERAL]

roo> addon search graph
roo> addon install id --searchResultId 01
```

And with that, you're ready to go. Most of the commands available to the Neo4j add-on are similar to the ones you've already seen with JPA. Let's set up your new project and the graph database:

```
roo> project --topLevelPackage com.crmco.crm
roo> graph setup --provider NEO4J --databaseLocation crmdata.db
```

Spring Roo will update the Maven dependencies to use the current Spring Data Graph and Neo4j version, as well as add an applicationContext-graph.xml configuration file which contains a single line of namespace-based configuration, shown below:

```
<datagraph:config storeDirectory="${neo4j.location}"/>
```

Now we can start to model our domain. Unsurprisingly, the syntax resembles the default Roo syntax for creating entities and adding fields:

```
roo> graph entity --class ~.model.Customer
roo> field string lastName
roo> field string firstName
```

These commands created the Customer entity class. But instead of having the @RooEntity annotation on top of the class (which would mark it as a JPA Entity), you can see that the addon added `@NodeEntity` which causes the AspectJ handling for the object graph mapping of Spring Data Graph to kick in:

```
roo> graph entity --class ~.model.Company
roo> field string company

roo> graph entity --class ~.model.CartOrder
roo> field date --fieldName dateOfOrder --type java.util.Date

roo> graph entity --class ~.model.LineItem
roo> field number --fieldName quantity --type int

roo> graph entity --class ~.model.Product
roo> field string name
roo> field string description
roo> field number --fieldName price --type double
```

Creating relationships is similar to adding references in a JPA-based domain model. Lets start with a simple relationship:

```
roo> graph relationship --from ~.model.LineItem --to ~.model.Product --fieldName
product
```

This adds a field to LineItem pointing to Product which is annotated with the direction of the relationship. Whenever this variable is read, Spring Data Graph looks for an outgoing "product" relationship of the LineItem node in the graph and returns the end node (i.e., a product). If you set the variable, a relationship is created. It is as simple as that:

```
@RelatedTo(direction = Direction.OUTGOING)
private Product product;
```

Creating a many-to-one relationship between `CartOrder` and `Customer` is simple:

```
roo> graph relationship --from ~.model.CartOrder --to ~.model.Customer --fieldName
customer --type ORDERED --cardinality MANY_TO_ONE
```

Adding the inverse relationship results in having a single customer field in the order with the type we provided at the command:

```
@RelatedTo(type = "ORDERED", direction = Direction.OUTGOING)
private Customer customer;
```

A bit more demanding is the relationship between `Customer` and `CartOrder`:

```
roo> graph relationship --from ~.model.Customer --to ~.model.CartOrder --fieldName
orders --type ORDERED --cardinality ONE_TO_MANY --direction INCOMING
```

Roo springs into action, adding a `Set<CartOrder>` orders field with the appropriate annotation to the `Customer` entity. Please note that this Set is auto managed, you never have to create it yourself and it will always reflect the relationships that exist in the graph. Any modification of the set will result in the appropriate modification of the graph relationships as well:

```
@RelatedTo(type = "ORDERED", direction = Direction.INCOMING)
private Set<CartOrder> orders;
```

Graph relationships are directed, but can always be traversed in the opposite direction. So if your domain model doesn't call for explicit relationships in either direction to model a domain concept, you should just use one relationship and specify the opposite direction at the other end.

Let's repeat that, with a twist.

This was the non-graphy way of modelling this domain. What if your line items are not much more than a relationship between orders and products? If there is no order, there is no line item. If there is no product, there is no line item for that too.

So instead of creating the line item as graph entity, we do the following:

```
roo> graph relationship --from ~.model.CartOrder --to ~.model.Product --via
~.model.LineItem --fieldName items --cardinality ONE_TO_MANY
```

The result of this operation unsurprisingly added a relationship field to CartOrder:

```
@RelatedToVia(direction = Direction.OUTGOING)
private Iterable<LineItem> items;
```

This time with a different annotation which annotates fields that don't return the target Node-Entity but rather the relationship entities in between. The iterator is read-only and can also handle millions of relationships between two nodes because of the lazy evaluation:

```
@RelationshipEntity
class LineItem {
    @StartNode CartOrder cartOrder;
    @EndNode Product product;
}
```

It also created a new class called LineItem but this time with a @RelationshipEntity annotation and two fields. One for CartOrder annotated with @StartNode and the other one for Product annotated with @EndNode. As of now, relationship entities cannot be created directly but rather via calling entity.relateTo(targetEntity) (e.g., cartOrder.relatedTo(product)).

Relationship entities can have fields too:

```
roo> field number --fieldName quantity --type int
```

After setting up the domain model, you're ready to go! Not bad for a few incantations, eh?

CHAPTER 2

Spring Roo on the Web

If you model your business data in the forest and nobody accesses it, did you really model it? In the last chapter, we looked at Spring Roo's sophisticated support for easy data modeling, but this is not an end in of itself. To be useful, you need to connect your applications to your users, and the most obvious way to do this today is to build a web application that they can interface with. Spring Roo provides excellent support here, as well. Spring Roo supports many web technologies, including Spring MVC, Spring Webflow, Flex, GWT, Vaadin, and Flex.

We'll review some of these technologies in this chapter.

Spring MVC

Spring MVC is a model-view-controller framework, which, as its name implies, has three essential parts. MVC is a well-known pattern in web frameworks. Its most redeeming quality is that it encourages clean, well-layered, decoupled applications that promote application growth to support new requirements. The "front controller" in the diagram is the Spring MVC DispatcherServlet, which needs to be registered in web.xml. It routes all requests coming into the web application to registered Spring MVC Controllers. Controllers are just POJO Spring beans that have annotations that describe the mapping between a URL (and the HTTP method—GET, PUT, POST, DELETE, etc.—used to access that URL) and the methods in a controller.

Controller methods are expected to process the request—perhaps access a backend service, invoke business logic, etc.—and then set up *model* (your JPA entities) data that's used to driven the generation of a *view*. The view—often—is a JSP page or some other sort of template, or it's a representation of some sort of data. This representation of data can be in XML, or JSON, or any other encoding you desire.

As Spring MVC uses Spring, it is completely configurable. Every aspect of it—from the view resolution mechanism, the views, the controllers, and the request dispatcher itself —can be configured. While Spring MVC is extremely flexible, it can be overwhelming for the uninitiated. By default, Spring MVC ships with common-sense defaults enabled,

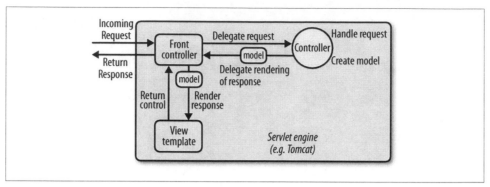

Figure 2-1. The interaction between the model, the view, and the controller

but building a typical application using Spring MVC can still be tedious because of all the technologies you're likely to want to integrate with it in order to build the best web application possible: JSPX for clean, XML-centric view templates, JavaScript to add dynanicism and interactivity to the client, HTML (which of course is used to describe the structure of the pages rendered in the browser), JSR 303-based bean validation to handle validation on your entities, REST (to expose clean, easily reused services in terms of the common idioms of the web), CSS to support declarative styling, Apache Tiles to support templating and page fragment reuse, internationalization, and much more. Spring Roo can be of great help here because it relegates all of these concerns to hushed whispers while you orchestrate your symphony.

Getting started with Spring MVC is a snap with Spring Roo. Let's take our first step and create a Controller to manipulate our Customer JPA entity:

```
controller scaffold --entity ~.domain.Customer --class ~.web.CustomerController
```

This command will take an unusual amount of time. The first time Spring Roo generates a web artifact for you, it automatically upgrades your Roo project to be a web project. Up until this point, Spring Roo was only building a .jar archive, not a .war. A .war archive requires a different directory structure, and configuration.

Sit back, and watch the fireworks. Spring Roo will set up a default web project that will install the correct configuration and numerous files that we'll reuse in the rest of the project, such as images, JavaScript assets, styles, and JSP tag libraries. It'll correctly update the Maven build to have all the dependencies that are required. We won't include the output here because there's simply too much. Try it out for yourself, and you'll agree: this is all code that you don't want to write yourself.

And, of course, Roo has generated a controller. Open up the Controller class, com.crmco.crm.web.CustomerController. Just as with the entities before, this class is spartan. Most of the magic is in the adjacent ITD files. You'll see two ITDs, one for the pureplay controller duties, and—surprise!—another controller to expose the data from the finder method we generated earlier.

Taking Our Application for a Spin

We'll dissect all of the newly generated code in a minute, but if you're anything like me, you're itching to see something working. Let's use the soothing, anti-itch salve of instant gratification and have a look at our application. If you've been following along in SpringSource Tool Suite, then this next bit's drag 'n drool simple: drag the project root in the Package Explorer on to the web server in the Servers tab on the bottom left.

 The server is called "VMware vFabric tc Server Developer Edition v2.5," which is quite a mouthful. We'll just call it tcServer Developer Edition, going forward. TcServer describes SpringSource's hardened, production and operations-friendly version of the leading Apache Tomcat 7 web server. TcServer Developer Edition, which comes bundled and preconfigured with SpringSource Tool Suite, is a free-for-development version of that product that comes bundled with all sorts of niceties, including sophisticated monitoring to help you profile and optimize your application during development. Naturally, you could use any other of the bundled WTP servers, including Tomcat, if you'd like, but I think you'll find tcServer Developer Edition a nice fit.

Once you've dragged the application onto the tcServer Developer Edition instance, start it by clicking on the green button with a white, right-facing arrow in the middle of it. It'll launch, and ask you if you'd like to enable Spring Insight to gather metrics, as shown in Figure 2-2:

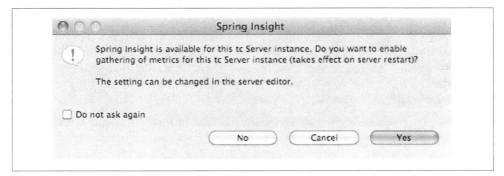

Figure 2-2. Spring insight dialog

Choose "Yes." The application should start up and be available at *http://localhost:8080/ crm/customers*. Figure 2-3 shows what this will look like.

Figure 2-3. Roo-generated web app

Pretty hot, right? What? Not a fan of the green? The look and feel is entirely custom-izable, and we'll address that shortly. But first, take a look around—click on some of the links. You can see that Roo's already generated forms so that you can search for customers, create them, update them, and list them. On the bottom of the page, you will see a few links where you can change the language displayed as well as the theme used. If you don't need these options, then they're easily removed, but it's nice to know they're already configured for you.

"You Win . . . a Braaand Neeew Web Application!"

Not really. Quite the opposite, actually. If you've been using Spring in web development before, then this application's going to be very familiar. In fact, if you've ever written an application that's as sophisticated and as large as the application that's just been created for you, then you're very familiar with these technologies, because you've no doubt spent a lot of time in front of them. So, nothing new about it. Just the familiar technologies you already know.

For those of you who haven't seen an application that tackles as much as this one does, we'll review some of the highlights.

Let's look at what's been configured in the web.xml. Roo has registered a listener—ContextLoaderListener—that is used to hoist Spring application contexts into exis-tence. This is typically done to hoist into existence application contexts whose beans are visible to all other contexts. You might, for example, use this to start up the appli-cation context that contains your services, data sources, and other beans that might need to be shared across multiple other contexts.

Roo has registered the DispatcherServlet, which is of course the central class not only in Spring MVC, but Spring's entire web stack. The DispatcherServlet can also hoist Spring application contexts into existence. You might register several DispatcherServ lets in a single application—one for Spring MVC, one for Spring Web Services, etc., as your needs demand, so beans registered in an application context by a `Dispatcher Servlet` are often web-tier and `DispatcherServlet`-specific in nature, and are often in service to that particular `DispatcherServlet`. It also knows how to enlist beans of certain types defined in the application context in specific types of service. For example, a `HttpRequestHandler` is a very low-level type of Spring bean that can be used in responding to HTTP requests.

Roo's also registered a few error-page elements to map an Exception and a 404 to the appropriate (preconfigured) Spring MVC resources.

Roo has registered several filters for us, to handle many different issues:

`HttpMethodFilter`
> Of the HTTP verbs—`PUT`, `GET`, `DELETE`, `POST`, etc.—your average browser only knows two of them, `GET` and `POST`. This filter is a proxy that adapts requests coming from a form in a browser using known conventions into the appropriate invocation on the server side.

`OpenEntityManagerInViewFilter`
> This filter keeps a JPA `EntityManager` open while requests are being served by Spring MVC. This lets you navigate the relationships on your JPA entities in the view tier, eschewing the dreaded `LazyInitailizationException` that you'd normally get if you didn't have an active session open.

`CharacterEncodingFilter`
> Allows one to specify a character encoding for requests. Current browsers typically do not set a character encoding, even if specified in the HTML page or form, so this is a convenient way to sanitize requests.

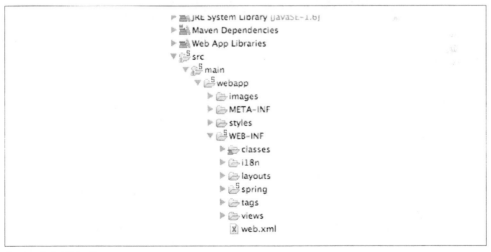

Figure 2-4. Web directory structure

Spring Roo has also generated a slew of layout code. The layout code's neatly organized in several directories, the kind of meticulous neatness you'd expect from a team leader with years of experience in scalable application development practices. Let's look at some of these directories in depth, particularly those under `src/main/webapp/WEB-INF/`:

Directory	Description
WEB-INF/i18n	This file contains the internationalized messages for your application. Spring makes it very easy to access internationalized messages anywhere.
WEB-INF/layouts	Where you should keep your Apache Tiles layout definitions (not the individual fragments that are arranged into layouts)
WEB-INF/spring	Suggested (though not required) folder for your Spring configuration files.
WEB-INF/tags/forms	Self-contained directory for tags that can be used to bind backing model objects to form fields. You can modify these fields (with some very small provisos) and Spring Roo will tolerate them. These tags also embed Dojo JavaScript where appropriate to provide client-side interactivity.
WEB-INF/tags/menu	Self-contained directory for tags to display the menu and navigation for your application.
WEB-INF/tags/util	Self-contained directory for tags to handle common scenarios like loading JavaScript, theming, and wrapping blocks in panels.
WEB-INF/views	Directory where common fragments used across all your pages—like footers and sidebars and so on—are stored, as well as fragments for individual pages, in nested folders.

Not too shabby! There's a lot here, and—as we'll see—it can all be tailored to spec, and in keeping with best practices typical of enterprise Java application development. All of this was generated (this one time) just to support the controller that we asked Roo to generate for us. Which brings us back around to the rabbit that got us down this particular hole in the first place, our `CustomerController`, and the scaffolding it generated...

Scaffolding

One of the best parts about Spring Roo—a framework that knows so very much about your domain model—is that it can use that knowledge to inform how it creates the web tier. The most natural extension of this idea is of *scaffolding*. Scaffolding, as it's famously called in Ruby on Rails and Groovy and Grails, describes the generation of views designed to manipulate the entities created.

Scaffolding is useful for a number of reasons. First, scaffolding views cuts the development time in half, getting you to a point where you can start prototyping a system and entering data. Sure, no automated tool's going to generate the *perfect* web application for you, but nobody said it would. Instead, it'll generate a web application, built to the highest standards in Spring web development, that you can then iteratively push to the finish line, changing the code as you go.

In running the controller scaffold command, we told Spring Roo to generate code to support the creation, update, and deletion of the Customer entity that we generated. It happily obliged, filling in all the gaps required to get our plain old Java project converted into a web application, and generating the required Spring MVC controller and supporting web views. The controller is presented below in its entirety:

```
package com.crmco.crm.web;

import com.crmco.crm.domain.Customer;
import org.springframework.roo.addon.web.mvc.controller.RooWebScaffold;
import org.springframework.stereotype.Controller;
import org.springframework.web.bind.annotation.RequestMapping;

@RooWebScaffold(path = "customers", formBackingObject =
Customer.class)@RequestMapping("/customers")
@Controller
public class CustomerController {
}
```

Just as with the entities before this, the controller that Spring Roo's generated for us is remarkably underwhelming. We can see a few telltale annotations of the same sort as were on the entities, specifically the @RooWebScaffold annotation, which is another marker annotation that signals to Roo that you want to "opt-in" to the services that Roo can provide. Specifically, the scaffolding provided by Spring Roo lives in an adjacent ITD, called CustomerController_Roo_Controller. Open that up and you can see that Roo's generated all sorts of controller methods. These controllers methods are used in conjunction with the JSP pages that Spring Roo's generated.

The scaffolding isn't a one-way trip. You can, for example, change the path attribute in the RooWebScaffold annotation, and the path referenced in the scaffolding ITD will update accordingly in all of the places it's referenced. You might, for example, change the path to say "clients," instead, and your entire web application—including the web tier artifacts—will update appropriately. Note, however, that it's left the old directory, views/customers/ in place for the web tier artifacts, and simply added a new directory in the same folder called views/clients.

As we've seen before, Spring Roo is very intelligent about how it balances its mandate to automate as much of the required code as possible with your (natural) wish to exert control on certain aspects of the application. When building the domain model, Spring Roo uses the clean separation of concerns enforced by the ITDs and the Java classes to ensure that it never steps on your toes. The rules are simple, you can use the command line to generate Java, XML, or other artifacts that you're then expected to maintain. As you edit the Java artifacts, Roo manages the required boilerplate in an ITD file—usually adjacent to the artifact—which you are *not* expected to modify, or even consciously be aware of. The only time thereafter that Spring Roo will modify your Java code directly, for example, is when you explicitly ask it to, from the shell.

This separation is less clear on the web tier. In this case, Roo has generated user editable artifacts—the .JSPX files—that it will also need to maintain. In particular, when you update an entity, it will try to update the corresponding JSPX pages and controllers appropriately.

The first thing to note is the file extension—JSPX—which might be new to some of you. Roo generates XML centric JSP files, not the standard JSP files that are still so common, unfortunately. JSPX files are easier to restructure because they're valid XML, and they also comport enough information in their structure that Roo can do smart things about refactoring them, even if you've updated the view since it was first generated.

The second thing that strikes us is the sheer number of files. The page that contains the form to create clients lives in src/main/webapps/WEB-INF/views/clients/create.jspx. Open the create.jspx and—above all—don't panic. The few stanzas you see before you really are all the code required to display the page you saw in your browser. You're standing on the shoulders of giants here, and that should be comforting, but I suspect you want to know *why* this works, not just that it works.

When Roo created our application it created a file called src/main/webapp/WEB-INF/spring/webmvc-config.xml, which in turn configures the Spring MVC framework. Roo's taking advantage of that aforementioned flexibility and has configured how Spring MVC resolves views. If you recall those scaffolding methods in the CustomerControl ler_Roo_Scaffold.aj, they all had return statements with strings, like this:

```
@RequestMapping(method = RequestMethod.GET)
public String CustomerController.list(
 @RequestParam(value = "page", required = false)
  Integer page,
 @RequestParam(value = "size", required = false) Integer size,
 Model uiModel) {
    ...
    return "clients/list";
}
```

This string—"clients/list"—is a bit of indirection. It's used by Spring MVC to resolve the view, but it doesn't specify a specific asset. Instead, it specifies a logical view name, which the configured view resolves can resolve accordingly. In this case, Roo's configured a TilesView on a URL view resolver, and configured a few Apache Tiles template definition files. These templates define the "shell" of the page—the navigation, header, footer, etc. The only thing that changes on all requests is the bit in the middle—the content unique to each URL. When Tiles looks at these indirect, logical view names, it resolves them to views that can be used to flesh out the missing part of the template. In the case of the "create" page, it loads "clients/create.jspx." So that's why the form's missing any evidence of any of the other stuff on the page.

Even so, the page has very few lines to support what looks like a complex form. But these tags may be novel to you. They are part of the assortment of tags that came with the code-generated Spring Roo application. If you'd like to exert control over how forms look in Spring Roo, then you can simply modify these tag files and you can exert control through the entire application. In essence, Roo's made it easy for you to build a very modular view, quickly.

How Spring Roo Builds the Scaffolding

Spring Roo builds these forms based on the relationships that it can infer from the JPA mappings. Note that Spring Roo doesn't strictly rely on the JPA associations, instead it relies on a generic model of the relationships that Roo maintains. This generic model could conceivably be used by other addons to plug in other types of models besides JPA.

There are tags for all the common types of data types. Roo does a great job mapping data types to the appropriate tags for forms or for display: booleans get checkboxes, small strings get an input field, large strings get text areas, and dates are rendered using a Dojo-based JavaScript date-picker. Roo employs its knowledge about your domain model's relationships to correctly display a select form element for them (e.g., sets, and enums).

There is an empty label in the customer scaffolding form indicating that there's no company specified (Figure 2-5). It'll give you an icon that you can click, but this will fail, since there's no scaffolding to support creating company entities. Since Roo hasn't generated any scaffolding for our other entities, it can't do much to ensure that the customer has a company, which is a required entity. This is also evident when you create a new customer—the application blows chunks because the foreign key for the company is null. We can create some scaffolding for all the entities in one go with the following command:

```
controller all --package ~.web
```

Figure 2-5. Crm crud forms

Once that's done, redeploy and try the application again.

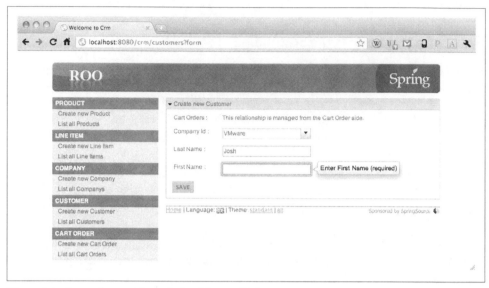

Figure 2-6. Create form with a relationship specified

Now, you'll see that the blue icon takes you to a resource where you can create a new company. Create one (say, "VMware," or "O'Reilly"), save it, and then return to the customers view. You'll see that the empty label's been replaced with a drop-down from which you can choose an entity.

 A note about redeployments. The tcServer Developer Edition WTP server instance will republish a deployed application anytime you change any of the resources or files. Any change will set this off, as long as you save the file you've modified. This behavior's unhelpful, most of the time. Double click on the WTP and make sure you've got the Overview tab selected. Expand the Publishing tab and choose "Never Publish Automatically." In this configuration, you'll have to manually restart the WTP instance whenever you'd like to see updates.

Usually, these redeployment cycles are trivial—Tomcat (and tcServer, which is based on it) enjoy the fastest deployment times of any enterprise Java servers. However, things could always be better, and SpringSource Tool Suite can help out here, too. Enable the "Application Reload Behavior" found in the same dialog box. This functionality gives you near instantaneous redeployment without ever restarting the server. This is a lot of power for one little checkbox!

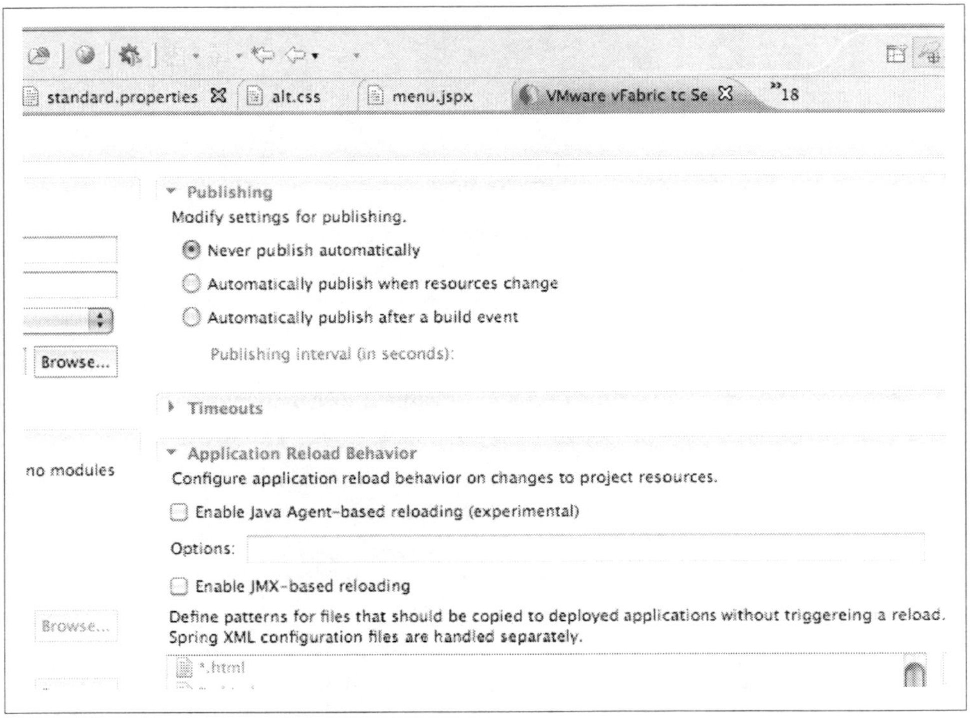

Figure 2-7. STS agent reloading and publishing

Now you've got a fully working system to create and manage your entities. Each entity has a page ("/list") that displays a grid of the available entities, and there are forms to view individual entities, create new ones and update or delete existing ones. Spring Roo's resilient to changes, too. Open up the Customer entity and add a new Date field. You can use the command line, as before, or simply type in the following:

```
@NotNull @DateTimeFormat(style = "S-") private Date birthday;
```

Save the entity and then watch the console; Spring Roo will update all of the existing scaffolding code. You'll need to also update the database table with the new column. Issue this SQL on the console.

```
alter table customer
    add column birthday date not null;
```

Redeploy. A new date picker widget will be visible on the form. You can reorder the fields of the form in src/main/webapp/WEB-INF/views/customers/create.jspx.

Spring Roo will *not* override your changes, but it will still correctly add new ones when you change the entities. The secret Roo's flexibility is the z attribute on the form field elements.

```
<field:datetime
    dateTimePattern="${customer_birthday_date_format}"
```

```
        field="birthday"
        id="c_com_crmco_crm_domain_Customer_birthday"
        required="true"
        z="3+6q083ESYHcRPLijiOzV7iRvjU="
    />
```

It's a hash that Roo calculates, based on the element name (name only, not namespace), attribute names present in element, attribute values present in the element. As long as this hash doesn't change (which is true as long as you don't do anything to change the identify, as described by this hash, of the element), then Roo can safely make changes to the element while you change everything see about the form, including position in the form and the surrounding HTML. If you make a change to the element manually, Spring Roo will notice this and update the "z" attribute to the value "user-managed." Roo doesn't manage all views in a project; typically it just manages the artifacts under the src/main/webapps/WEB-INF/views folder, and the menu.jspx file.

We're a fair bit into this little book of ours, and we've learned a lot, but it's worth noting just how much effort it would take to rebuild this entire application, soup to nuts:

```
persistence setup --database H2_IN_MEMORY --provider HIBERNATE
database reverse engineer --package ~.domain --schema PUBLIC
controller all --package ~.web
```

In addition to the above command line invocations, we also modified the Customer entity's Java class directly, but you could just as easily have used the Roo command line to add those fields. All in all, we've achieved a lot for so very little.

Spring MVC's got a lot of redeeming features that make it the most powerful web framework available to the Java developer today. Its annotation-driven programming model, the out-of-the-box abstractions to handle every manner of view (Tiles, PDFs, CSV and Excel spreadsheets, images, RESTful payloads like JSON and XML, etc.), its robust support for requirements typical of any serious Java application, all contribute to Spring MVC's appeal.

Spring WebFlow

Spring MVC applications, by default, don't require an HTTP session. For many applications, an HTTP session is an extra weight that adds no value. The one place where HTTP sessions are valuable is in dealing with transient, client-specific state that has to be propagated across multiple requests. You might, for example, use an HTTP session to store the state associated with a shopping cart and checkout process. Typically such processes require the skilled management of object state over a series of several pages; they require foundational support for navigating backwards and forwards, much like a state machine. This sort of state is difficult to manage, however. There can only be one HTTP session associated with a client, no matter how many requests are made, which of course has the makings of a classic concurrency problem. Sessions are a shared resource. Spring WebFlow provides a framework specifically for managing problems like this.

You can install Spring WebFlow quickly by issuing the following command:

```
web flow
```

Spring WebFlow builds on top of Spring MVC, and shares common configuration and dependencies. Spring MVC and Spring Web Flow work well together, providing a powerful combo-punch for all the challenges you might face. The majority of your application will typically be developed in Spring MVC, with Spring WebFlow filling in the gaps where you need stateful, "conversational" interaction. Spring WebFlow, once configured, works by reading in descriptions of "flows," described using Spring name-spaces. These flows describe how pages in should be strung together in sequences.

Let's look at the sample flow and folder that's created when you install Spring Web Flow.

```
<?xml version="1.0" encoding="UTF-8" standalone="no"?>
<flow xmlns="http://www.springframework.org/schema/webflow" xmlns:xsi="http://
www.w3.org/2001/XMLSchema-instance" xsi:schemaLocation="http://
www.springframework.org/schema/webflow http://www.springframework.org/schema/webflow/
spring-webflow-2.0.xsd">
    <view-state id="view-state-1" view="sampleflow/view-state-1">
        <transition on="success" to="view-state-2"/>
        <transition on="cancel" to="end-state"/>
    </view-state>
    <view-state id="view-state-2" view="sampleflow/view-state-2">        <transition
on="cancel" to="end-state"/>
    </view-state>

    <end-state id="end-state" view="sampleflow/end-state"/>
</flow>
```

The flow contains three meaningful stanzas: two `view-states`, and one `end-state`. These are only two of the many types of states that Spring WebFlow provides. Each state describes itself—in this case a view-state describes a view to dispatch to—as well as the transitions it might take. Spring WebFlow resolves views in the same way as Spring MVC, and here the values for view—`sampleflow/view-state-2`., and `sampleflow/view-state-1` -map to Apache Tiles definitions, which in turn map to the JSPX files, just like the strings returned from controller methods in Spring MVC. SpringSource Tool Suite provides fantastic support for visualizing Spring Web Flows, just click on the "flow-graph" tab at the bottom of the editor panel when this flow is open. It produces a visualization of the graph. This visual view of the graph is editable; you can add new nodes to the graph by dragging elements from the pallette on the left onto the graph or alter the graph nodes by double clicking on the them and modifying their properties.

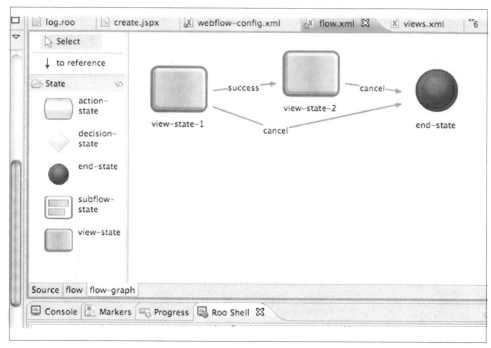

Figure 2-8. Webflow visualization

The specifics of Spring WebFlow are beyond the scope of this book, but getting started is easy—simply install the configuration from here, and then consult the comprehensive documentation at *http://www.springsource.org/go-webflow2*.

Integrating Roo with other Web Frameworks

Spring Roo is an enabler—a gateway drug. It simplifies to the point of triviality the configuration and installation of technologies in service of your application. As powerful as Spring Roo is, it does not do its work alone. It relies on the Spring framework and other, sister frameworks to provide the runtime functionality—to actually make these integrations work, to make them meaningful. As we move through the next section, remember that Spring itself has integrations with more technologies than any other technology and that half of the work of surfacing these technologies in Spring Roo is often just having a way to enable the integration in a Roo project. The best integrations, however, offer ways to improve development-time productivity with these technologies. In this section, we'll take a look at a few web frameworks that provide compelling integrations for Roo users.

Some of the most exciting integrations today are in the web framework space. People are building dynamic, highly interactive applications today that are a rich mix of client side technologies like JavaScript, CSS, HTML, or Flex, and server side technologies like Spring MVC.

For the integrations in the rest of this chapter, let's assume a known starting point. Delete your project, and create a new one using the New Roo project dialog in Spring-Source Tool Suite (**File > New > Spring Roo Project**) and reset the entities with the following Roo shell commands before trying out the technology specific commands:

```
persistence setup --database H2_IN_MEMORY --provider HIBERNATE
database properties set --key database.url --value jdbc:h2:tcp://localhost/~/roo_crm
database reverse engineer --package ~.domain --schema PUBLIC
```

GWT

The first technology on our rich-client roundup is the Google Web Toolkit, or GWT. GWT is a cross compiler—it takes Java syntax code and compiles it into JavaScript. The libraries available to the developer using this cross compiler resemble a subset of the Java standard libraries, as well as several Java abstractions that are essentially mirrors of the common APIs that you would access running JavaScript in a browser, like the DOM.

To add new functionality to a GWT application, you can build complex abstractions using Java, or you can write JSNI—JavaScript Native Interface—adapter code and provide a Java binding for it. This has been used by many to, for example, expose the ExtJS JavaScript library as a Java API which can then be used in GWT code.

The GWT provides a convenient way for Java developers to build highly interactive, dynamic JavaScript applications with rich, client-side state. GWT applications may communicate with the server using a type of serialization that GWT recognizes.

Writing large, rich, cross-browser applications is easy with GWT. Java's built in support for encapsulation and reuse lends itself to larger codebases. The JavaScript that GWT produces is very optimized—it's as if you had the most intelligent JavaScript coder writing your code for you. The Java-to-JavaScript compiler can do things that you'd never do if you were writing JavaScript directly, including function inlining and obfuscation. The result is JavaScript code that's blazing fast, if a bit ugly to look at.

To use GWT successfully, you need to set up the appropriate Eclipse plugins, configure GWT itself, and then connect your server side services to the client-side code.

To get started, simply run the following command:

```
web gwt setup
```

This single command takes care of everything and leaves you with a working GWT-based UI for your entities, in much the same fashion as the original Spring MVC application. Below is a screenshot. You can restart the Spring application inside of tcServer, and then start the GWT client side code itself. SpringSource Tool Suite already has all the Google plugins pre-configured to support development with GWT. Your

Maven builds already been configured to correctly compile the GWT application code as well. To test your GWT code, open up the GWT entry point—an XML file at the root of your Roo base package (com.crmco.crm.ApplicationScaffold.gwt.xml—and right click on it in the Source code editor window. Choose Run As > Web Application. This will launch a browser with your code. During development, GWT runs in "hosted mode." Hosted mode is an environment that lets GWT connect your code to the IDE (and the debugger). To support Hosted Mode, you need a plugin in your browser that can communicate back to your IDE. You will be prompted to install this plugin if you don't already have it when you first run this application.

The application should look something like this:

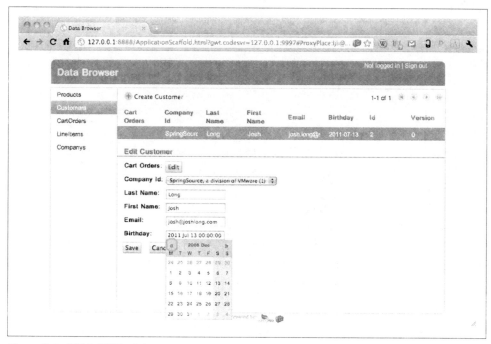

Figure 2-9. CRM-GWT editing

SpringSource Tool Suite includes all the sophisticated tooling to support development with GWT. Indeed, the Google plugin that comes prebundled with SpringSource Tool Suite also supports other Google technologies, like Google App Engine. Incidentally, Spring has the distinct position of being the only enterprise Java framework that works portably on all the major cloud environments, including Google App Engine, Amazon Elastic Beanstalk, and of course, CloudFoundry. The Google plugin includes a visual designer for GWT, which you can use by clicking on a GWT XML artifact and then clicking on the "Design" tab at the bottom.

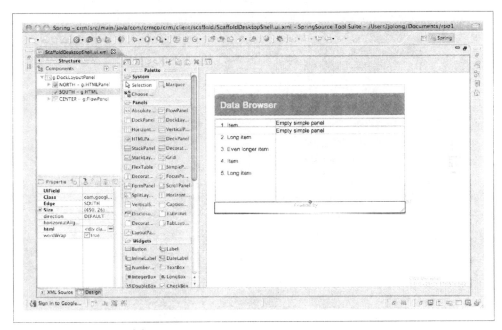

Figure 2-10. *GWT visual designer*

GWT is an example of SOFEA -- service oriented front end applications. In an SOFEA application, clients make requests against server side resources to activate business logic and marshal server side state back and forth using dumb objects (which smells suspiciously like a DTO). This has the benefit that server side state is kept to minimum, assuming of course that the services invoked are stateless as well. However, the resulting code is filled with much more boilerplate code and more prone to security concerns.

Vaadin

Vaadin is different. Vaadin is built on top of GWT, and comes with a large array of components, but these components are different than typical GWT widgets. Vaadin widgets, as run on the client side, are simply stateless "proxy" widgets that delegate all their business logic (and state management) to a server side peer. Thus, Vaadin applications make a lot more calls to the server, and the server keeps all the UI state, not the client as with GWT. Because all the business logic runs on the server side, and because all the UI state exists on the server side, the client needs only to be responsive and to convey state changes to the server. Keeping the important business logic on the server simplifies things a lot—it means you can avoid tedious code to serialize Java objects back and forth as JavaScript objects, and any concerns about security are minimized because all the business logic runs on the server side, away from prying eyes.

A cursory examination of the code in our previous GWT example will reveal a lot of boilerplate code. Roo certainly got the ball rolling for us, but if the code it generated is any indication, then there's a lot of code to be written for a typical GWT application. Vaadin solves this problem by providing a rich set of components and framework code that greatly reduces the developer footprint.

To use Vaadin with Spring Roo, you first have to install it. It is not shipped out of the box with Spring Roo, but instead is part of the huge, ever expanding ecology of Spring Roo addons.

```
pgp trust --keyId 0xBF0451C0
download accept terms of use
addon install bundle --bundleSymbolicName com.vaadin.spring.roo.addon
```

Once this is done, you can now start using the Spring Roo Vaadin addon. Issue the following command to have the Roo addon generate scaffolding for our entities, in the same way that we used the MVC and GWT addons to generate scaffolding.

```
vaadin setup --applicationPackage ~.web --baseName crm --themeName crm --
useJpaContainer false
```

This will install Vaadin, add the required Java dependencies, update web.xml (*http:// web.xml*), etc. It installs some helper and utility code in the com.crmco.crm.web package. Inspect that package and you'll see a handful of classes, a far cry from the reams of code implanted by the GWT addon. Let's see what Vaadin can do for us in terms of scaffolding. Run the following command to generate CRUD forms.

```
vaadin generate all --package ~.web.ui --visuallyComposable true
```

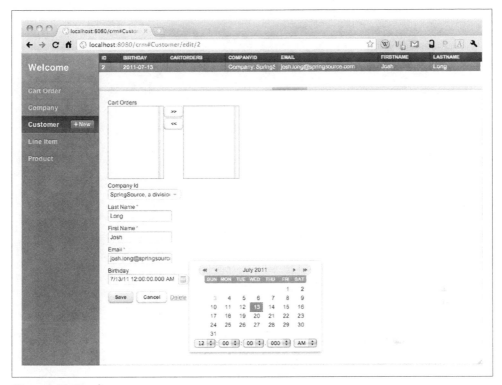

Figure 2-11. Vaadin crm

The generated Vaadin application is pretty striking, and doesn't take a lot of code! Vaadin also has a visual designer that you can use. You need to add the Vaadin Eclipse plugin to SpringSource Tool Suite. In SpringSource Tool Suite, go to Help > Install New Software, and in the "Work With:" field, enter the URL of the Vaadin Eclipse update site, *http://vaadin.com/eclipse*. Select the "Vaadin" tree, and install everything. Follow the prompts. Once everything's configured, you can open any Vaadin form in the Vaadin visual designer. Right click on the `com.crmco.crm.web.ui.CartOrderForm`, choose Open With > Vaadin Editor. If you find yourself looking at source code, then look at the bottom of the editor pane and click on the Design tab. You should be shown a visual approximation of the design, just as with the GWT designer. You can select elements and modify them in the visual tool, as well.

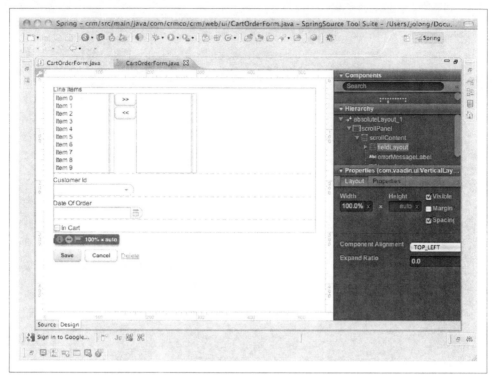

Figure 2-12. Vaadin visual designer

Where to go from Here

While we haven't covered all the supported technologies, there are numerous other addons that support Flex, Wicket, and many other technologies.

Many of these technologies—like Flex, GWT, and Vaadin—are geared specifically to form-intensive, rich-client-type applications, and not to being a general purpose web framework like Spring MVC. We think you'll find that most applications are best served by introducing Spring MVC (and perhaps Spring WebFlow) as the base, and then—as islands of richer, page-centric functionality are required—by introducing something like Vaadin.

CHAPTER 3

From Prototype to Production

If you've got this far, then you already have a working application with a working entity model as well as a powerful, tried and true web framework. You've got everything you need to take your application well past the prototype stages and develop it into a viable, production worthy application. The devil, as they say, is in the details. But fear not, Spring Roo can make short work of these tedious, but important, tasks.

In this chapter, we'll look at testing, securing and logging.

Logging

Logging is an integral part of your application. It provides the normative connection between your application and the rest of the world, during debugging, in testing, and in production. Logging should be integrated as frequently as possible. Spring Roo comes with the Log4j dependency already enabled. With one command you can install a Log4j configuration file, `log4j.properties`.

```
logging setup --level INFO
```

would for sample install a configuration file setup to handle logging at the INFO debug level.

Security

Ben Alex, the creator of both the Spring Security project and of Spring Roo, joked famously about the progression of the configuration required to add Spring Security configuration to a Spring application. In earlier versions of SPring Security—which was released as Acegi Security in 2003—the configuration could be quite burdensome. Today, Spring Security provides a XML namespace as well as intelligent configuration options and factory beans, making its installation a trivial matter. However, it can be simpler. As Ben would note, Spring Roo reduces the required configuration to one, solitary line.

Spring Security is widely considered the most powerful security framework available to Java developers. It has a *lot* of power, and can readily meet most security challenges. Spring Roo provides a sane way to get the basics taken care of, quickly. For our purposes, we simply want to secure our web application.

You must have configured a Spring MVC application, otherwise the security commands will not be available on the shell. To get started, type:

```
security setup
```

This command packs a lot of punch. It's added the appropriate Spring Security Maven dependencies to the pom.xml file, it's added a new Spring configuration file (src/main/resources/META-INF/spring/applicationContext-security.xml), it's added a login.jspx page, and a new Tiles definition (view.xml). It's also added the Spring Security servlet to web.xml (*http://web.xml*), and configured extra URL protection in webmvc-config.xml.

The salient configuration lives in the applicationContext-security.xml, presented below.

```xml
<?xml version="1.0" encoding="UTF-8"?>
<beans:beans xmlns="http://www.springframework.org/schema/security"
    xmlns:beans="http://www.springframework.org/schema/beans"
    xmlns:xsi="http://www.w3.org/2001/XMLSchema-instance"
    xsi:schemaLocation="http://www.springframework.org/schema/beans http://
www.springframework.org/schema/beans/spring-beans-3.0.xsd
    http://www.springframework.org/schema/security http://www.springframework.org/
schema/security/spring-security-3.0.xsd">

    <!-- HTTP security configurations -->
    <http auto-config="true" use-expressions="true">
        <form-login login-processing-url="/resources/j_spring_security_check" login-
page="/login" authentication-failure-url="/login?login_error=t"/>
        <logout logout-url="/resources/j_spring_security_logout"/>
        <!-- Configure these elements to secure URIs in your application -->
        <intercept-url pattern="/choices/**" access="hasRole('ROLE_ADMIN')"/>
        <intercept-url pattern="/member/**" access="isAuthenticated()" />
        <intercept-url pattern="/resources/**" access="permitAll" />
        <intercept-url pattern="/**" access="permitAll" />
    </http>

    <!-- Configure Authentication mechanism -->
    <authentication-manager alias="authenticationManager">
        <!-- SHA-256 values can be produced using 'echo -n your_desired_password |
sha256sum' (using normal *nix environments) -->
        <authentication-provider>
            <password-encoder hash="sha-256"/>
            <user-service>
                <user name="admin"
password="8c6976e5b5410415bde908bd4dee15dfb167a9c873fc4bb8a81f6f2ab448a918"
authorities="ROLE_ADMIN"/>
                <user name="user"
password="04f8996da763b7a969b1028ee3007569eaf3a635486ddab211d512c85b9df8fb"
authorities="ROLE_USER"/>
```

```
        </user-service>
      </authentication-provider>

    </authentication-manager>
  </beans:beans>
```

The http element describes which roles may access which URLs. The access attribute on the intercept-url elements uses Spring Expression Language statements to specify which tests to run when unauthorized access is requested. Questions about the qualifications of a request are delegated to an authentication-manager, which you can see configured below. Like all things in Spring, the authentication-manager is pluggable through an SPI. For the common cases, the namespace provides help. You can, for example, configure authentication against a database, or a single-sign on system like CAS, or OpenSSO.

Once this configuration is in place, you can more granularly restrict access to specific fragments of pages. For example, you might wish to restrict which menu options are shown to people in the menu. Open up the menu.jspx page, and then add the JSP tag namespace for the Spring Security tag.

```
xmlns:sec="http://www.springframework.org/security/tags"
```

For the specific parts of the page that you wish to restrict, enclose it with this new tag, like this:

```
<sec:authorize ifAllGranted="ROLE_ADMIN">
  ...
</sec:authorize>
```

With these simple changes, we've already introduced URL-security, login managment, and page-fragment security. A full introduction to Spring Security is out of the scope of this book, but you might consider consulting the excellent Spring Security documentation at *http://static.springsource.org/spring-security/site/index.html*, or the excellent PACKT book, *Spring Security 3*.

Testing

We've gotten very far, very quickly, because we've relied on Spring Roo to do the right thing (TM). Since it does, unfailingly, we haven't had to worry about testing, thus far. But Spring Roo is very amenable to testing, it encourages it. Spring Roo fully supports round tripping and wants to make it as easy as possible to support testing code so that —as we introduce code that varies from the script, so to speak, we don't risk introducing errors.

When creating entities, you can eaisly add integration tests for the created entities by appending the --testAutomatically to the command, like this:

```
entity --class ~.domain.Customer --testAutomatically
```

You can add the integration tests retroactively, too, if you forget to specify this option at creation time or you had the classes generated using database reverse engineering.

```
test integration --entity ~.domain.Customer
```

This will generate an integration test (`src/test/java/com/crmco/crm/domain/Customer IntegrationTest.java`). This integration test is a standard unit test. There's an adjacent unit test aspect, `CustomerIntegrationTest_Roo_IntegrationTest`, that contains unit tests for all the properties on the entity, as well as the finder methods.

You can easily generate unit tests for all the other entities. You can run the unit tests in SpringSource Tool Suite by right clicking on the unit test and selecting Run As > JUnit Test. When you build the code on the command line using Maven, the unit tests will be run automatically.

Integration tests are the most typical type of unit test, but not the only one. Roo also supports mock tests, as well as interaction testing with Selenium.

Mock testing describes the practice—nay, the *art*—of testing interactions between APIs by delegating API calls to dumb objects that record the interactions and check that they meet test expectations. You can create simple mock test, quickly, like this:

```
test mock
```

This will create a single mock test, which you can then build on.

Interface testing—the final frontier in unit testing—is one of the hardest types of testing to get right, and also one of the most worthwhile because the user interface layer in an application can be host to a lot of complex state management. A user interface also has a lot of logic that is business critical, and that is not served by traditional unit tests. Interface tests provide an effective way to test this logic by simulating user interactions and measuring that the behavior of the user interface is in accordance with the expected behavior.

There are several projects that provide support for these kinds of tests, including HttpUnit, HtmlUnit, and Selenium. The first two frameworks simulate requests against a web application in terms of HTTP requests (very low level) and in terms of manipulation of a web page's document object model (mouse clicks, button presses, etc.). While HtmlUnit has a lot of potential, it is ultimately a Java simulation of the browser, not the browser itself. Selenium is different. Selenium works as a plugin in the various browsers and then surfaces a sophisticated API to "drive" the browser using those plugins. It should not be surprising then that Spring Roo makes it very simple to build Selenium tests.

Roo can generate your Selenium test for any controller, like this:

```
selenium test --controller ~.web.CustomerController
```

This modifies the Maven configuration for the project and installs support for the Maven plugin:

```
<plugin>
    <groupId>org.codehaus.mojo</groupId>
    <artifactId>selenium-maven-plugin</artifactId>
    <version>1.1</version>
    <configuration>
        <suite>src/main/webapp/selenium/test-suite.xhtml</suite>
        <browser>*firefox</browser>
        <results>${project.build.directory}/selenium.html</results>
        <startURL>http://localhost:4444/</startURL>
    </configuration>
</plugin>
```

This will generate tests for the controller in the src/main/webapp/selenium folder. You can run these tests through Maven using the following command:

```
mvn selenium:selenese
```

This will launch Firefox and run the tests for you.

Conclusion

Well, that brings us to the end of our hopping tour of Spring Roo. In the span of the wafer thin tome you hold in your hands, we've covered setting up a Spring application and working Maven build, addressing database persistence with JPA and Neo4j, building web applications using—among other things—Spring MVC, Spring WebFlow, GWT, and Vaadin, securing an application and testing an application. Imagine what we could do if we had written another ten pages!

We hope you've enjoyed this little tour, but don't worry—the fun doesn't stop here. If you want to learn more, we encourage you to check out *http://www.springsource.org/ roo*, where you'll find all sorts of information including documentation, tutorials, screencasts and news. Spring Roo's a quickly growing project, with new features added by the development team as well as the numerous third party contributors. If Spring Roo doesn't already have a feature that you need, then check back tomorrow! If it hasn't been addressed by then, then we encourage you to consult the forums as well as the JIRA for the project. The Roo team heavily prioritizes community feedback in deciding what to add next and always welcomes feedback.

Finally, if you want to learn more about the many individual technologies we've discussed in this book, hop on over to the SpringSource web site (*http://www.springsource .org*). SpringSource also has a YouTube channel, at *http://www.youtube.com/Spring SourceDev*.

Finally, you can find your humble authors on Twitter! Follow @SpringSource (*http:// www.twitter.com/SpringSource*), @starbuxman (*http://www.twitter.com/starbuxman*), and @smayzak (*http://www.twitter.com/smayzak*).

About the Authors

Josh Long is the Spring developer advocate for SpringSource, a division of VMWare; an editor on the Java queue for InfoQ.com; and the lead author on several books, including Apress' *Spring Recipes*, 2nd Edition. He is also a contributor to several open source projects, including Spring Integration, Spring Batch, Spring Hadoop, and the Activiti BPMN 2 project. Josh has spoken at many different industry conferences internationally including TheServerSide Java Symposium, SpringOne, OSCON, Java-Zone, Devoxx, Java2Days and many others. When he's not hacking on code for Spring-Source, he can be found at the local Java User Group or at the local coffee shop. Josh likes solutions that push the boundaries of the technologies that enable them. His interests include cloud computing (especially, CloudFoundry), scalability, BPM, grid processing, mobile computing and so-called "smart" systems. He blogs at blog.spring-source.org or joshlong.com.

Mr. Mayzak is part of the Cloud Applications Platform team at VMware. As part of this team he is focused on mapping our solutions to customers needs and ensuring that what we offer fits their requirements. He is constantly in the field working with customers on their Cloud initiatives.

Get even more for your money.

Join the O'Reilly Community, and register the O'Reilly books you own. It's free, and you'll get:

- $4.99 ebook upgrade offer
- 40% upgrade offer on O'Reilly print books
- Membership discounts on books and events
- Free lifetime updates to ebooks and videos
- Multiple ebook formats, DRM FREE
- Participation in the O'Reilly community
- Newsletters
- Account management
- 100% Satisfaction Guarantee

Signing up is easy:

1. **Go to: oreilly.com/go/register**
2. **Create an O'Reilly login.**
3. **Provide your address.**
4. **Register your books.**

Note: English-language books only

To order books online:
oreilly.com/store

For questions about products or an order:
orders@oreilly.com

To sign up to get topic-specific email announcements and/or news about upcoming books, conferences, special offers, and new technologies:
elists@oreilly.com

For technical questions about book content:
booktech@oreilly.com

To submit new book proposals to our editors:
proposals@oreilly.com

O'Reilly books are available in multiple DRM-free ebook formats. For more information:
oreilly.com/ebooks

O'REILLY®

Spreading the knowledge of innovators   oreilly.com

The information you need, when and where you need it.

With Safari Books Online, you can:

Access the contents of thousands of technology and business books

- Quickly search over 7000 books and certification guides
- Download whole books or chapters in PDF format, at no extra cost, to print or read on the go
- Copy and paste code
- Save up to 35% on O'Reilly print books
- **New!** Access mobile-friendly books directly from cell phones and mobile devices

Stay up-to-date on emerging topics before the books are published

- Get on-demand access to evolving manuscripts.
- Interact directly with authors of upcoming books

Explore thousands of hours of video on technology and design topics

- Learn from expert video tutorials
- Watch and replay recorded conference sessions

Spreading the knowledge of innovators   safari.oreilly.com

CPSIA information can be obtained at www.ICGtesting.com
Printed in the USA
BVOW060540041011

272710BV00010B/13/P